"The Mountain"

Michèle Vachon Beaudin

(c)2010 immi'ges & words press
All rights reserved

Prints can be purchased separately by contacting
us for princing and details.

Book Design by Michèle Beaudin

www.immiges.com
www.immigesandwords.com

michele@immiges.com

ISBN 978-0-615-33963-4

Library of Congress Control Number: 2009942145

Printed in the United States of America

First Edition

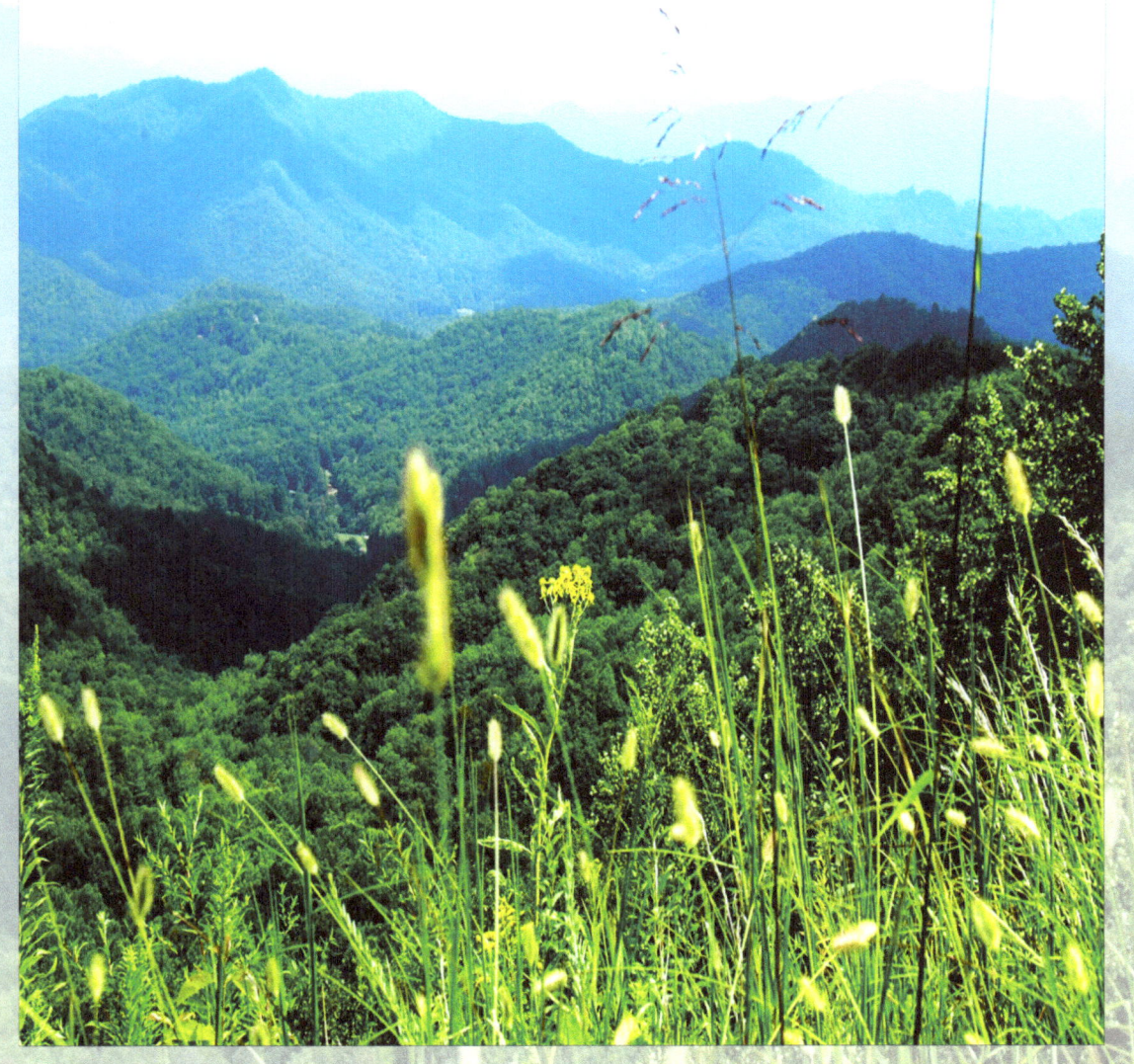

I'm on my way...
The mountain is beckoning.
As I climb from the valley against the river flow,
I soon find rapids, first, gently playing around the rocks,
then raging as the water tumbles from the falls.

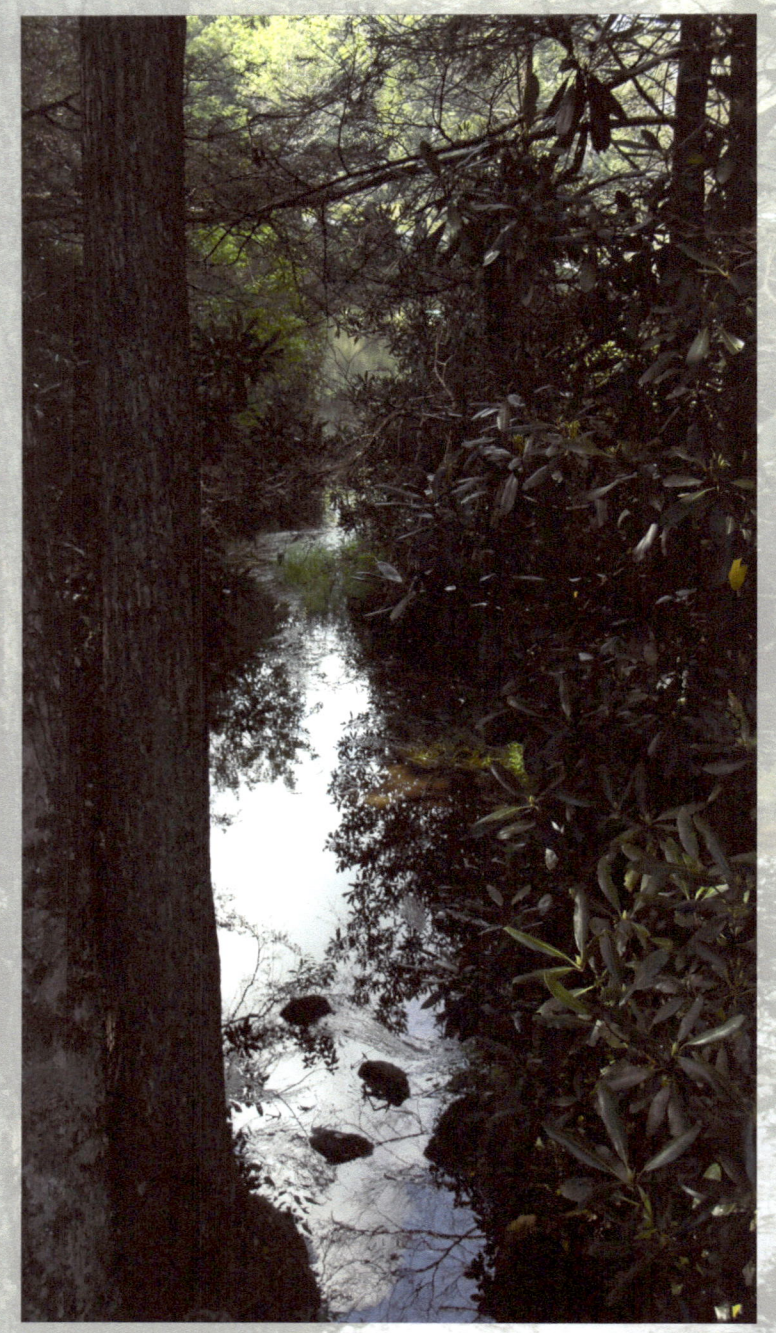

High up near the crest,
a winding trail
calls for me
to follow its course.

The path is teeming with
life where rocky hills
live in harmony
with flowers and wild life.

Sometimes, a creek
emerges and teases my
toes daring me to follow
its lead to its source
where it all began.

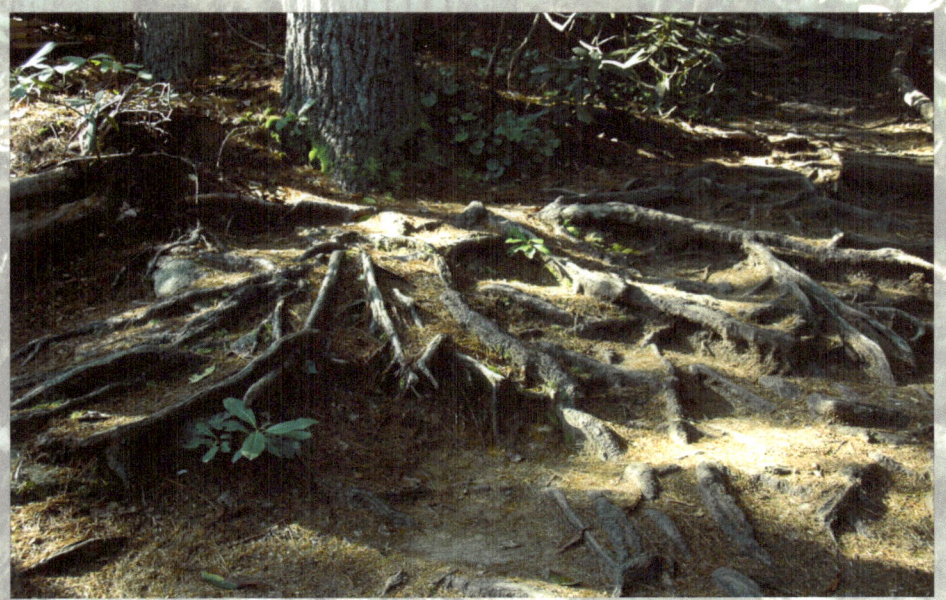

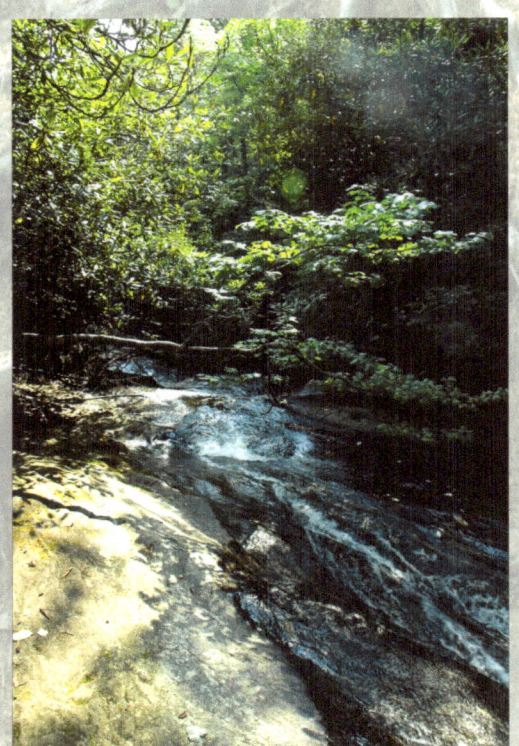

Now deep in the forest, the ground, first coated with decaying leaves and fallen branches, is now covered with gnarly roots and rocks.

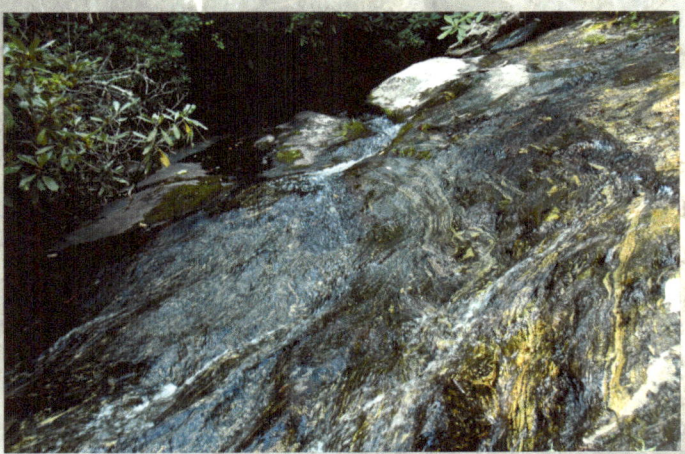

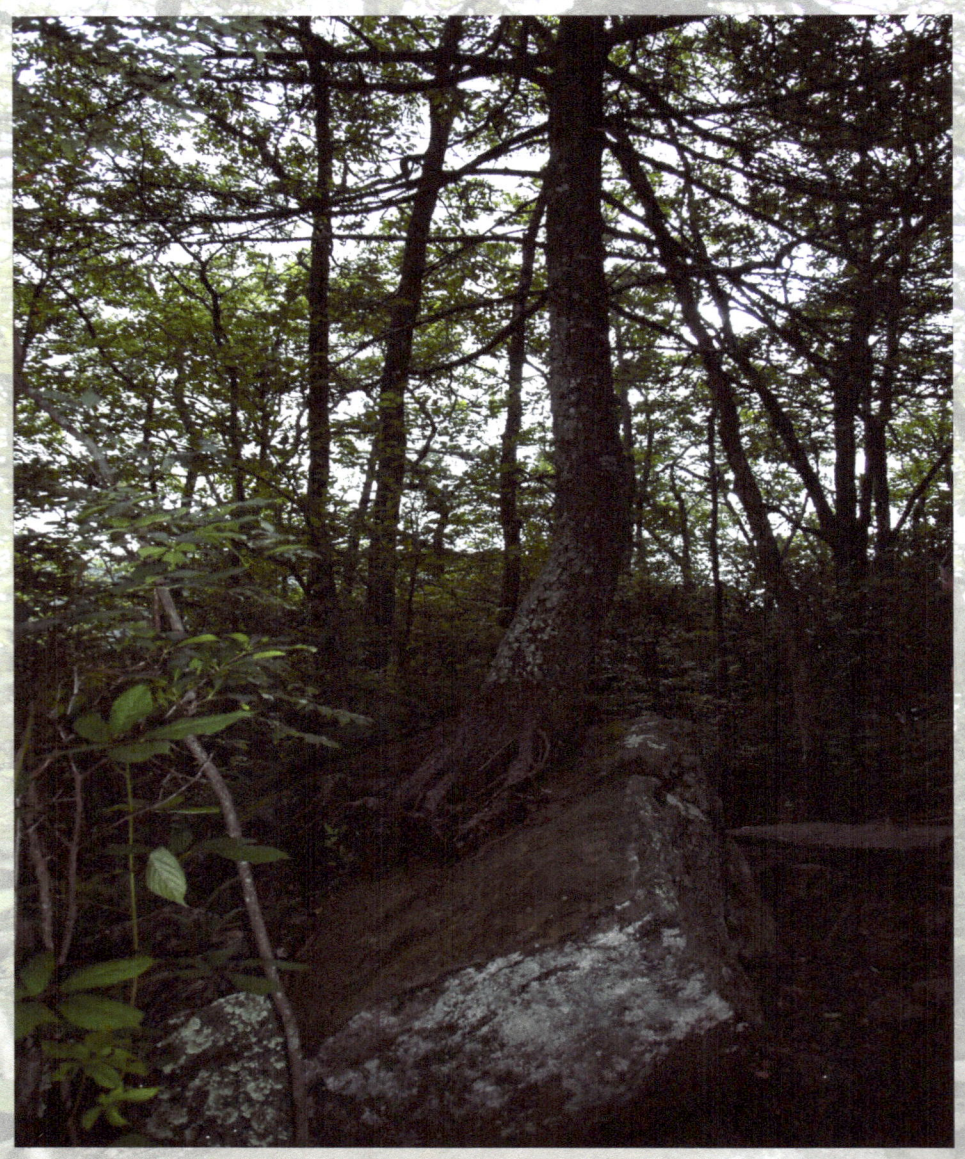

Around the bend, another miracle of nature awaits.
The ancient tree, dwarfed because it was born so high above
the sea, has survived winds, storms and snow
to stand witness to nature's endless bounty.

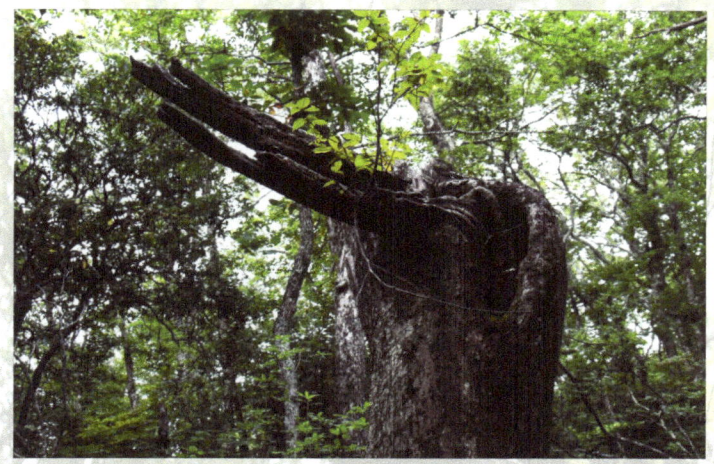

Along the path, trees spread
their arms out, each branch
a unique work of art.
Some soar and
reach for the sky, but
one stands out as if
sculpted to mock
the birds nesting
on its highest limb.
Then, there are those
that hide trails of treasures
yet to be discovered.

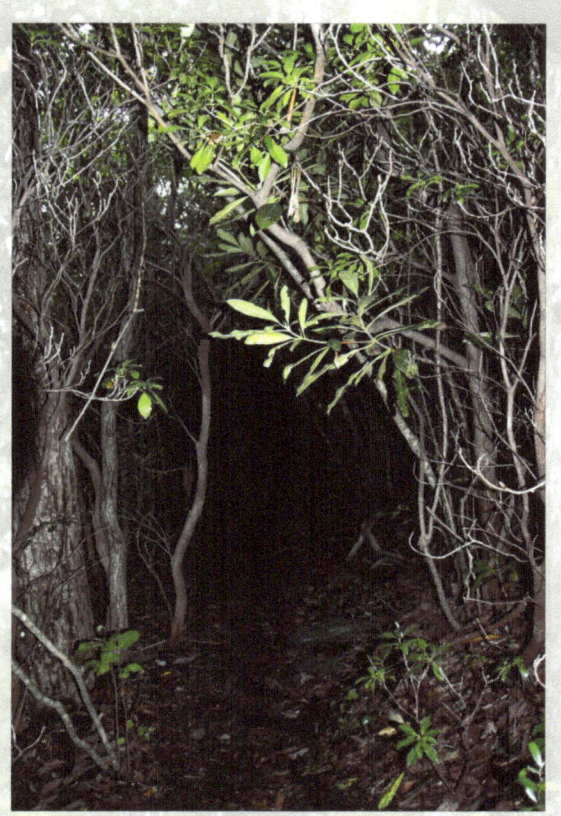

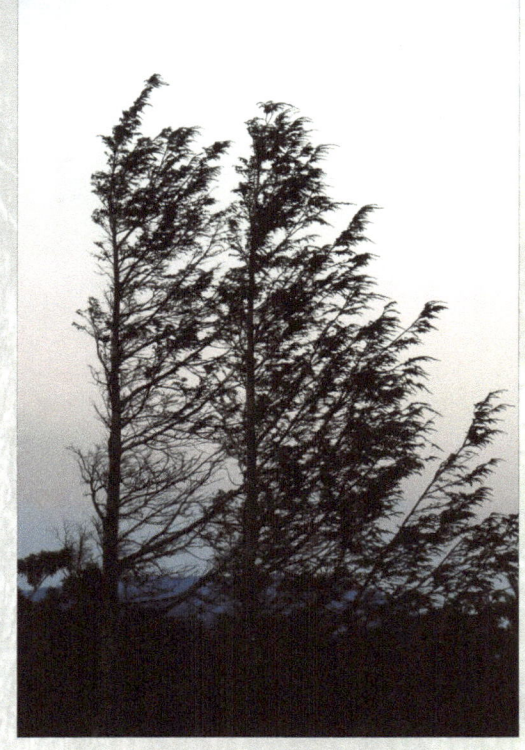

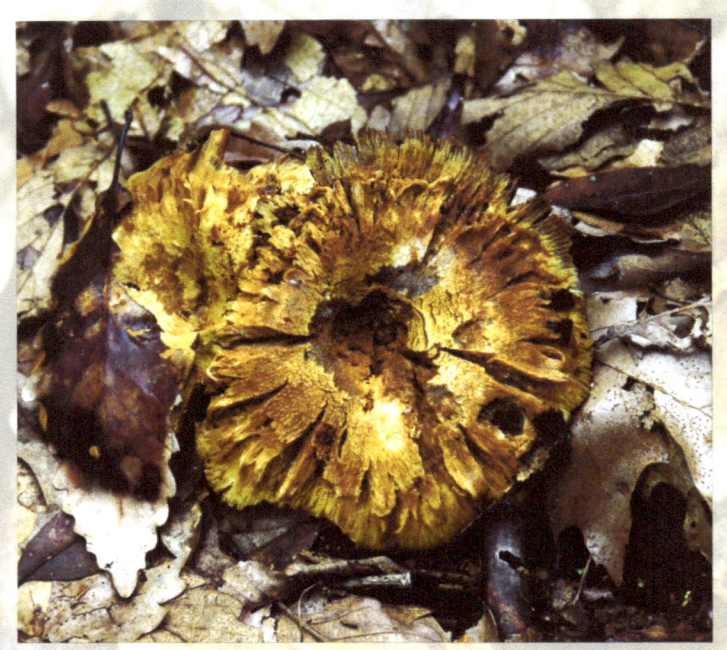

Life flourishes along the way.
Mushrooms, adorned
with brilliant colors,
rest on soft beds of
leaves like velvet cushions
holding precious jewels.

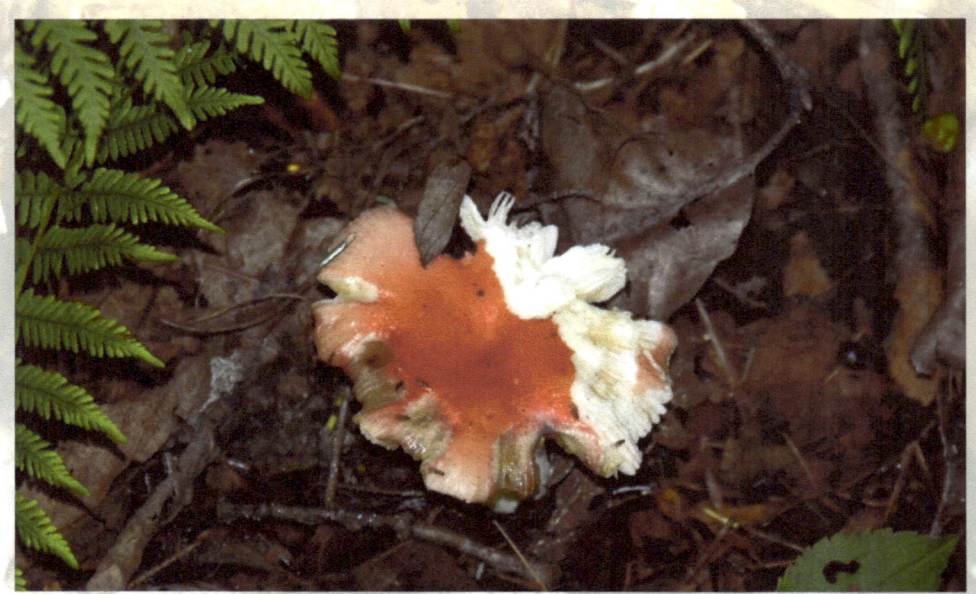

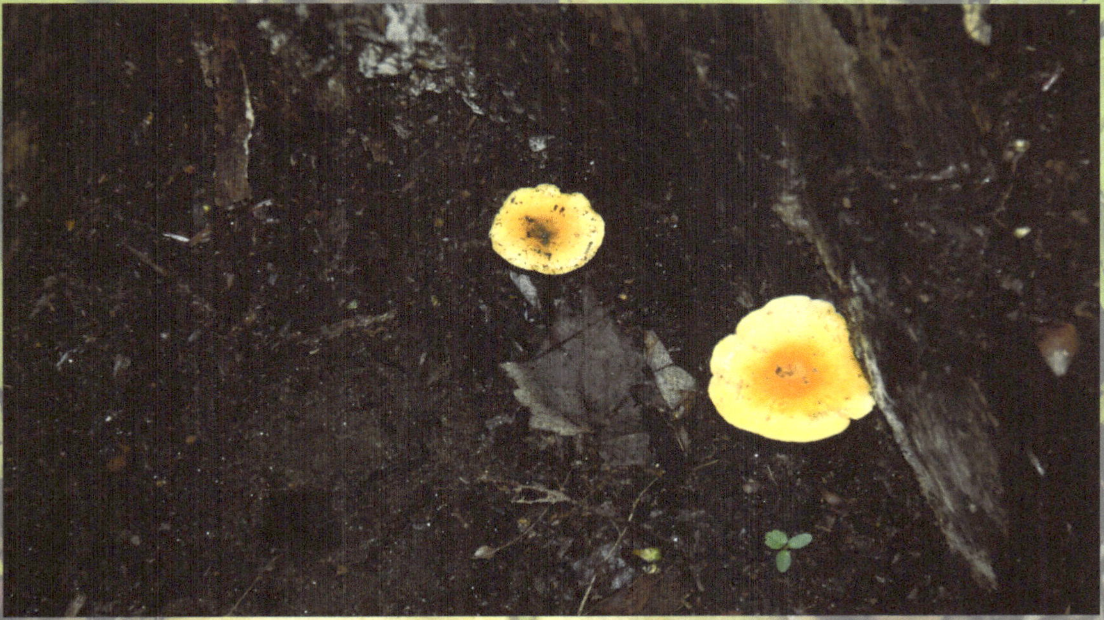

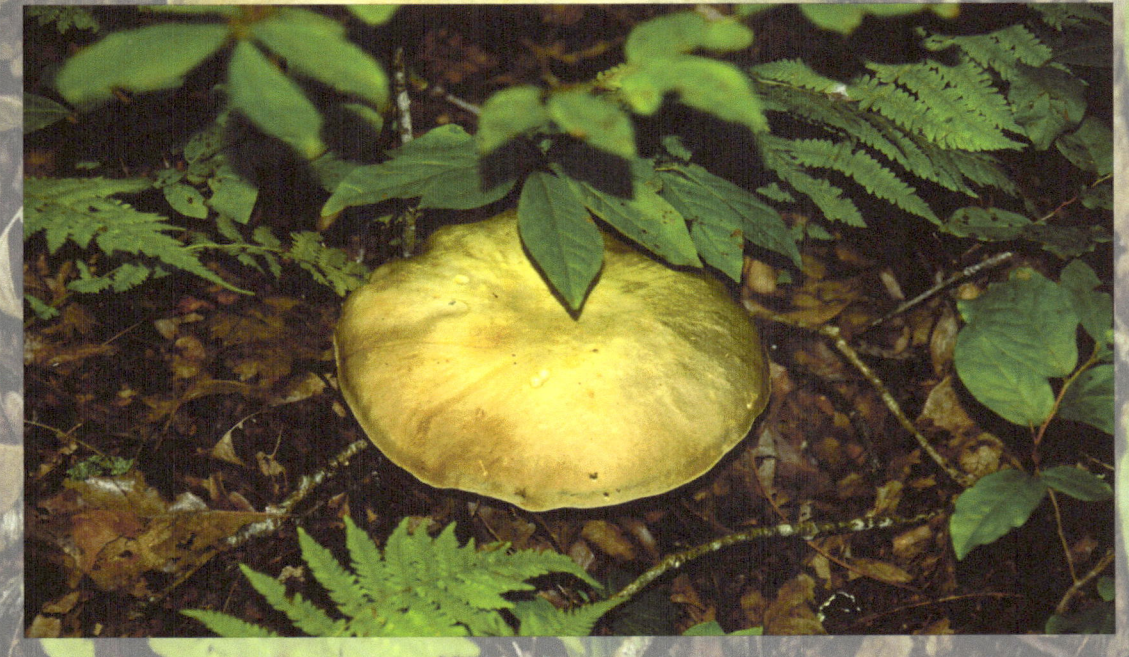

Dark and light, the path is all encompassing in its artistic display

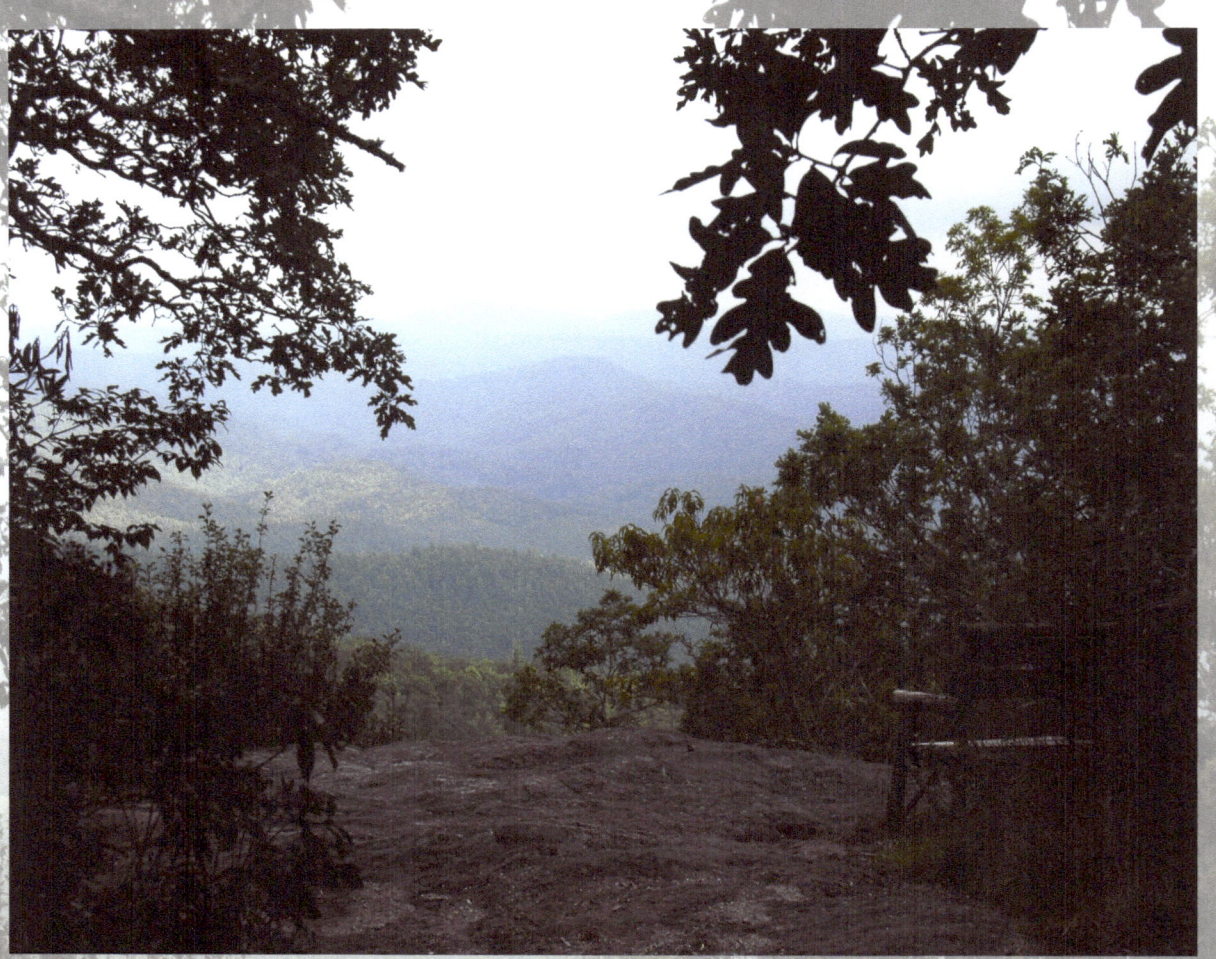

I follow the way back to the lodge.
The trail ends and layers of mountains
appear as far as the eye can see.
This is a place to meditate as the soul
seeks silence and peace.
Nature provides the wonderment
and human hands a rustic bench
where to rest.

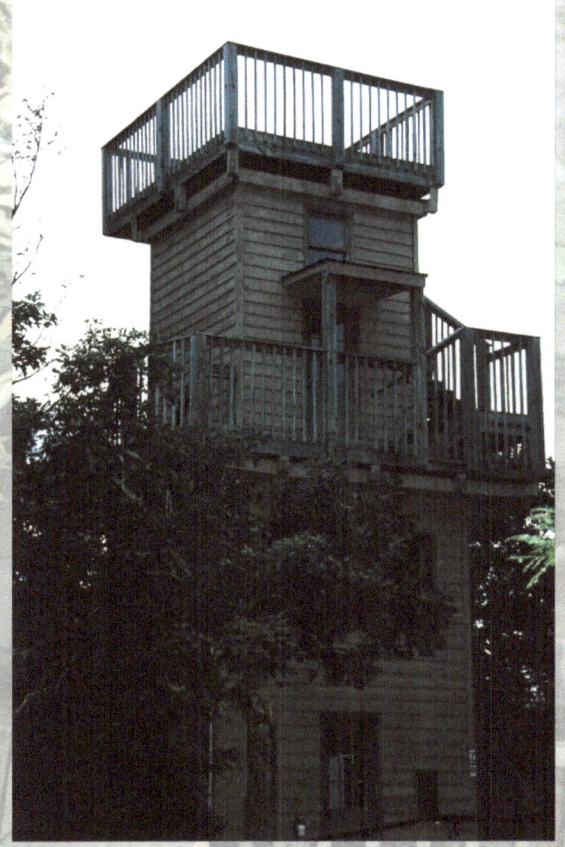

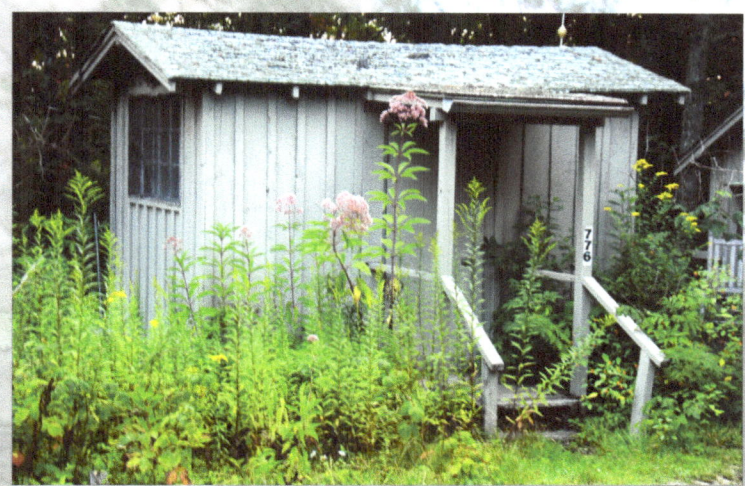

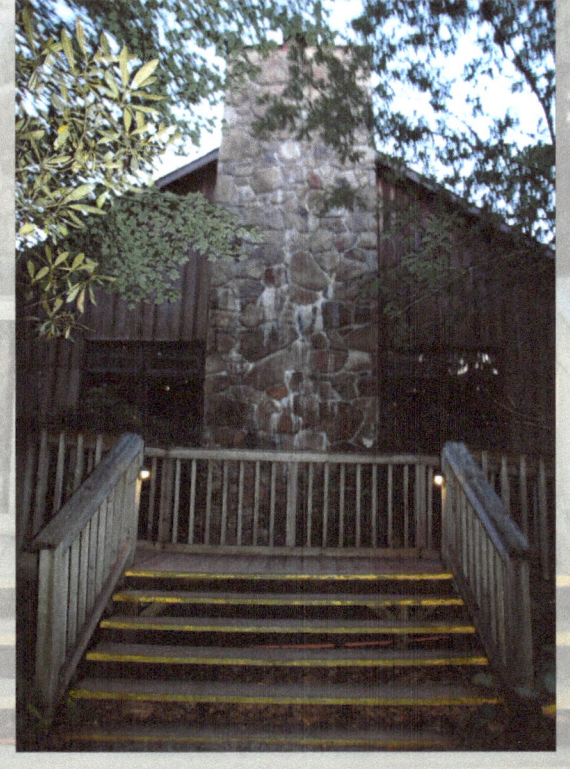

I have now returned to the haven
of The Mountain retreat,
surrounded by
like peace seeking souls.
A cabin, a rustic lodge,
a tower to see the sun set
and a rock to watch it rise.

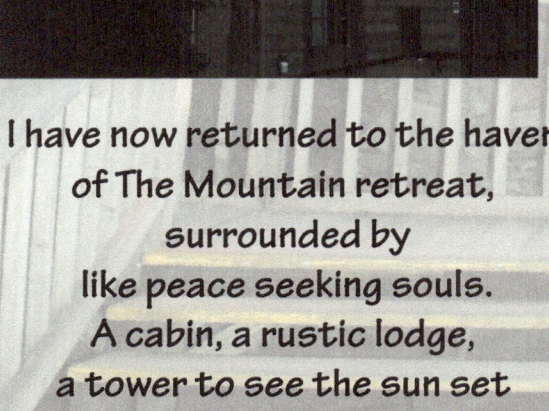

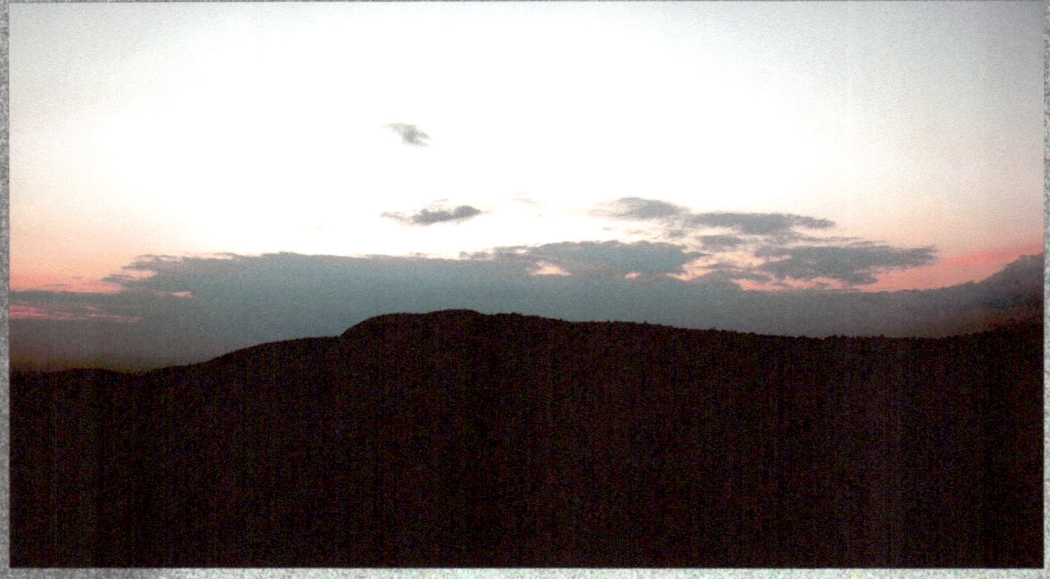

I climb up the tower, eager to see the sun set
behing the chain of hills.
Light fades while clouds move in
to carve designs into the evening sky,
just as the moon finds
a way to show herself high above the mountains.

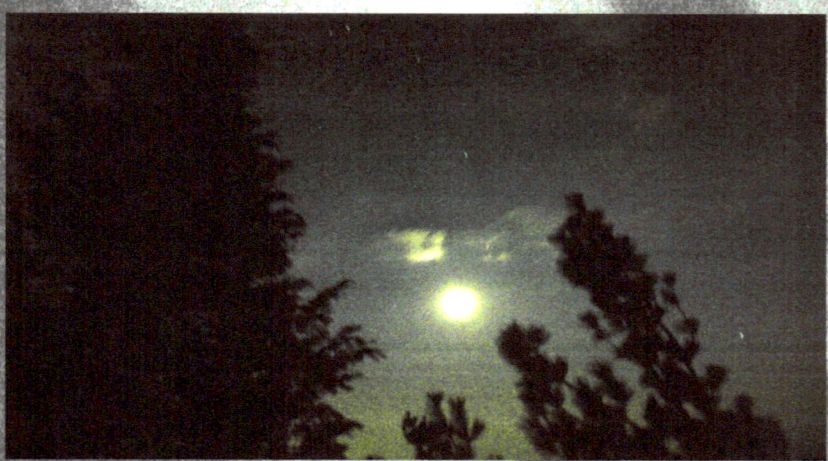

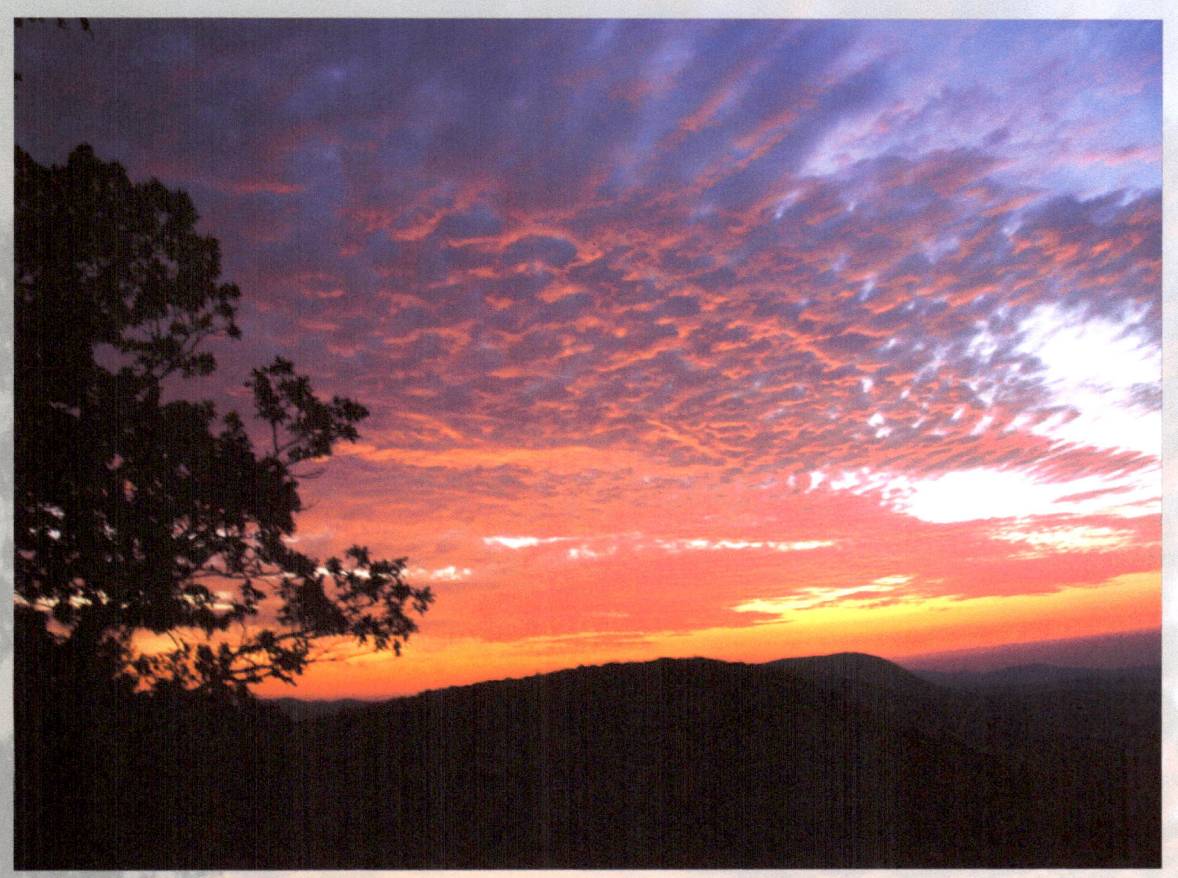

The path is still dark as I walk to meditation rock at dawn.
I reach my destination and witness the morning drama
already unfolding on a red canvas.
Clouds that form images of alligators in my mind,
are soon but skelletons, skin and bones
slowly detaching themselves from the bodies.
The north star becomes overshadowed by
the rising sun and I hear the first human sound of the day.
The precious moment has fleeted but I smile,
reminded that I am not alone.

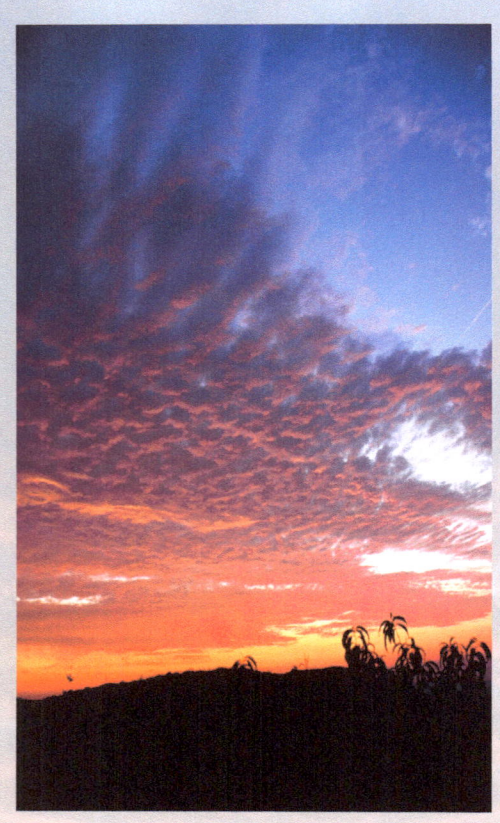

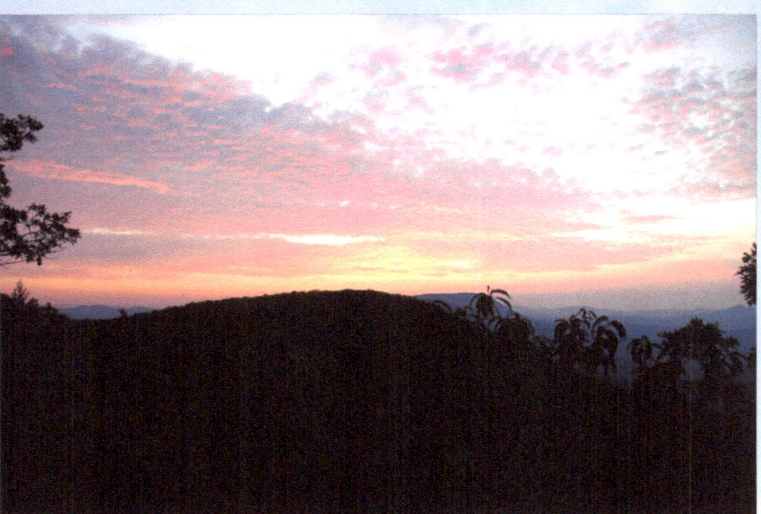

Witnessing the birth of a day.

**Clouds with scales
and claws soon turn
into gentle covers
shading the mountains
from the rising summer sun.**

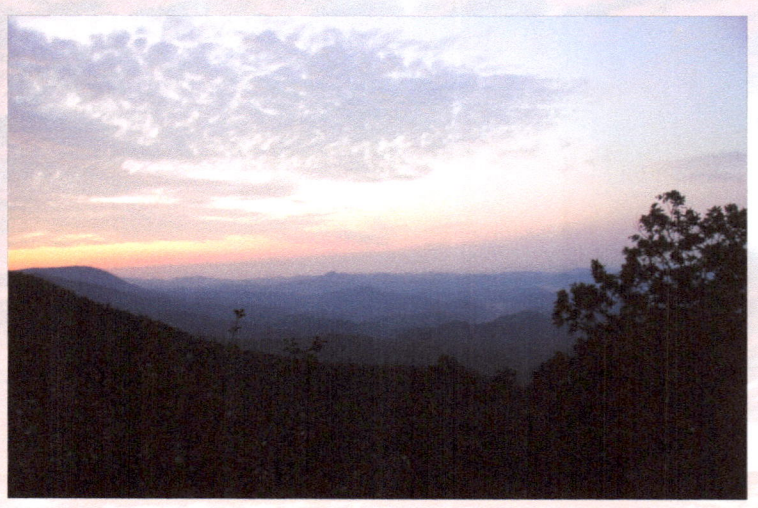

Another day to explore,
more surprises along the way.
A Labyrinth by the side
of the road calls for
me to follow its trace.
A black racer snake
slithers along the
the intricate circles
watchful of my footsteps.

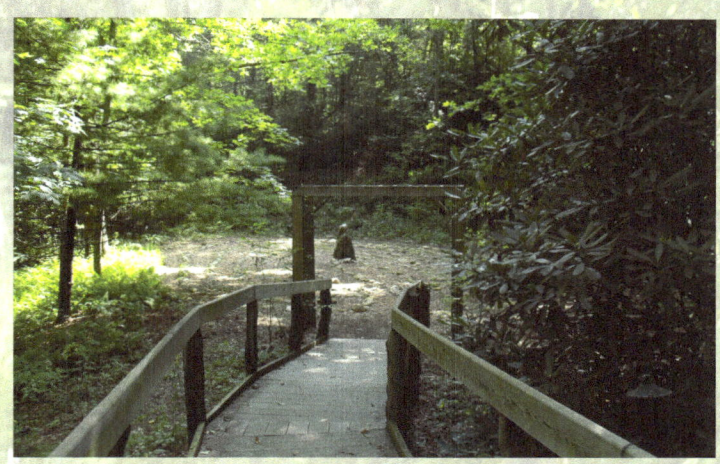

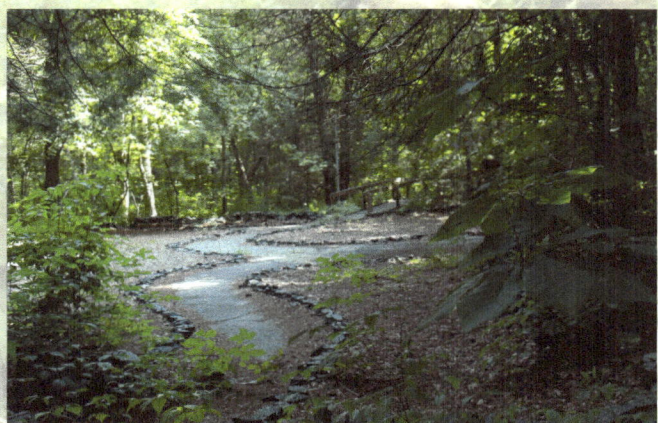

This Labyrinths is said
to provoke a
contemplative state
and calm the mind.

I soon lose
track of time
and the world
stands still,
bringing peace
and serenity.

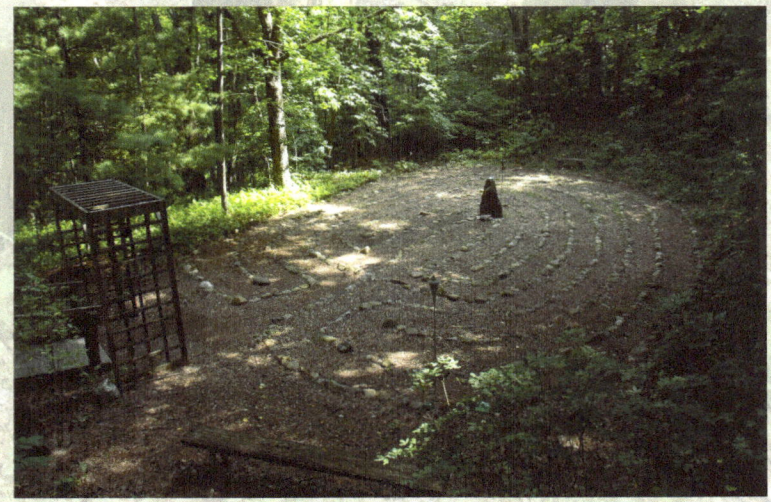

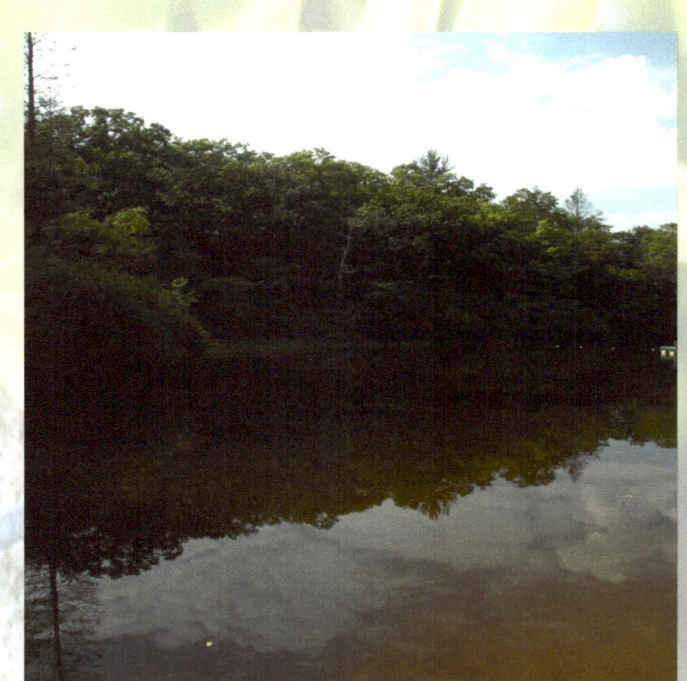

A lake appears
at the bottom of the hill.
Two dragonflies
vie for the same reed.

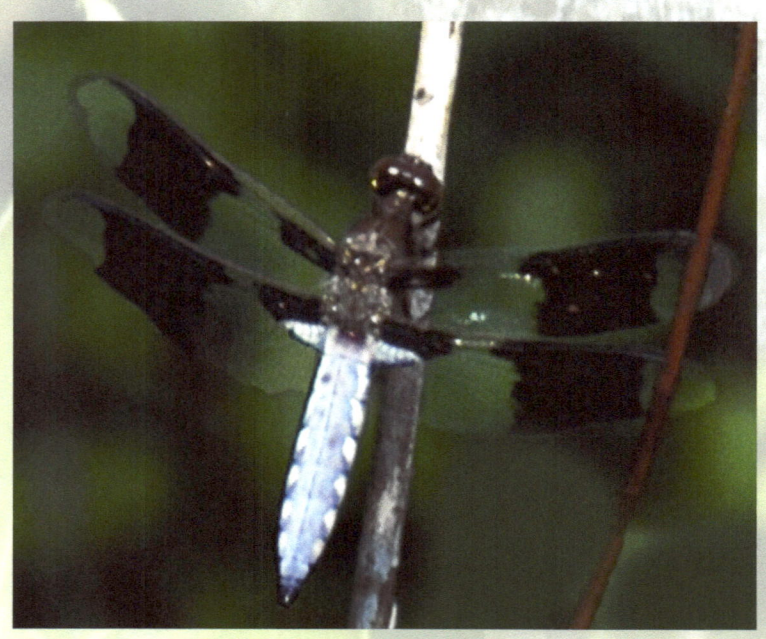

One finds a mate
and, like war planes
chasing the enemy,
they win the eternal
struggle faced by their
kinds every day.

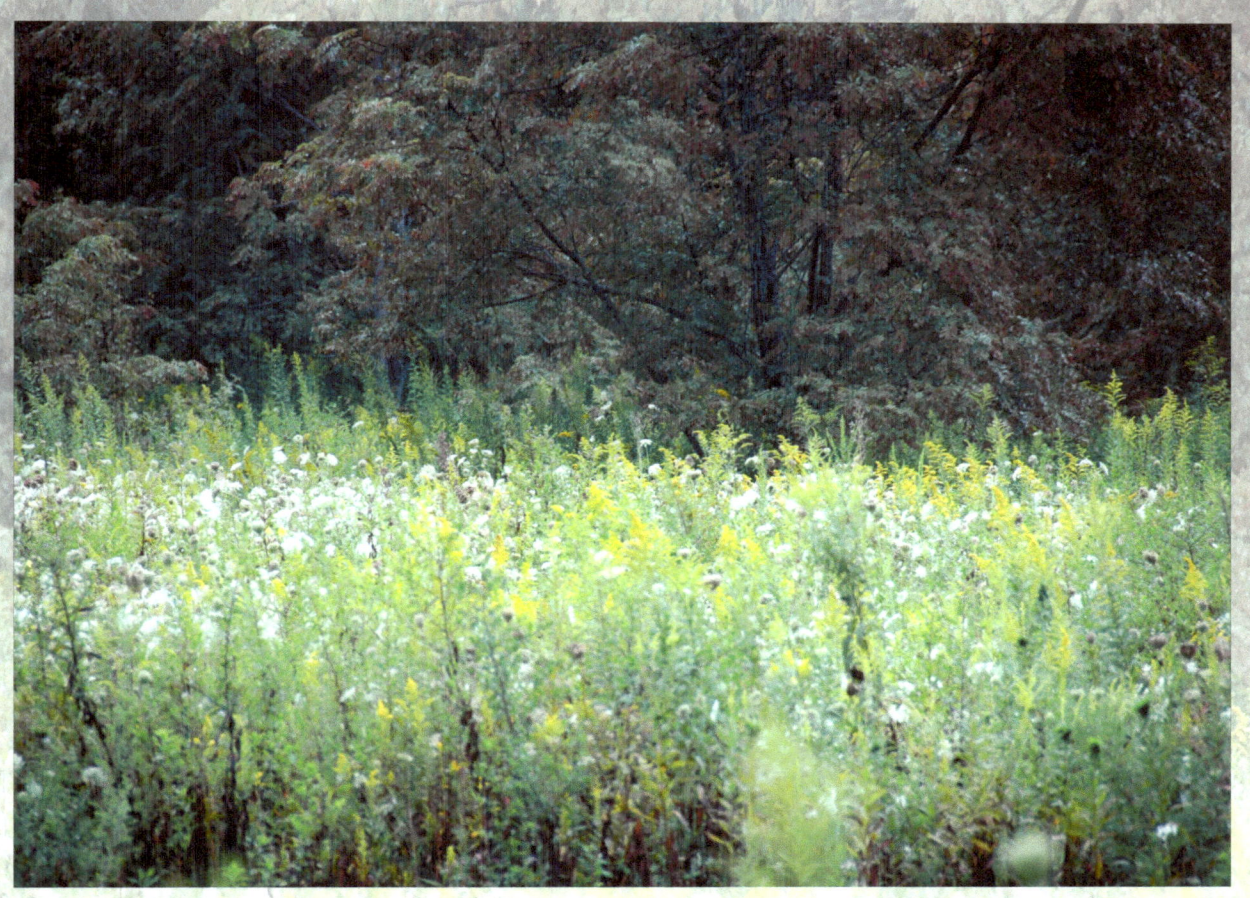

I rest by a clearing
on the way to the falls.
Wildflowers, heavy with pollen
and haunted by bumble bees,
give way to a lone rabbit,
frozen in its track,
startled by my human presence.

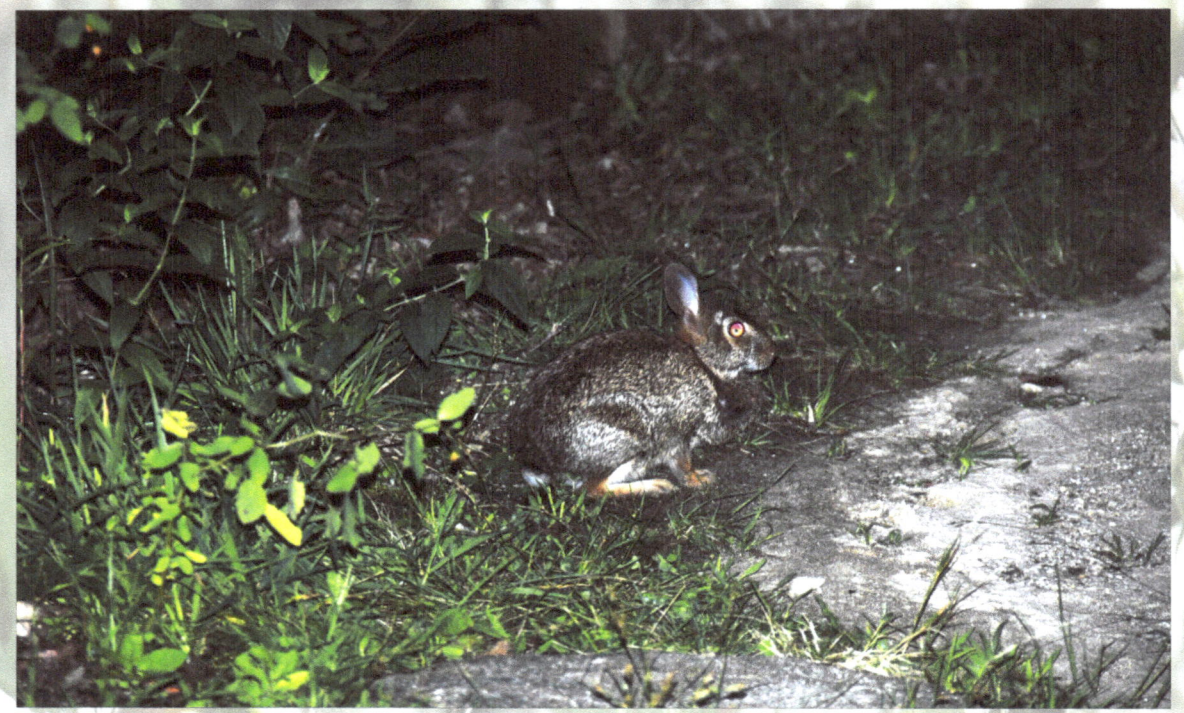
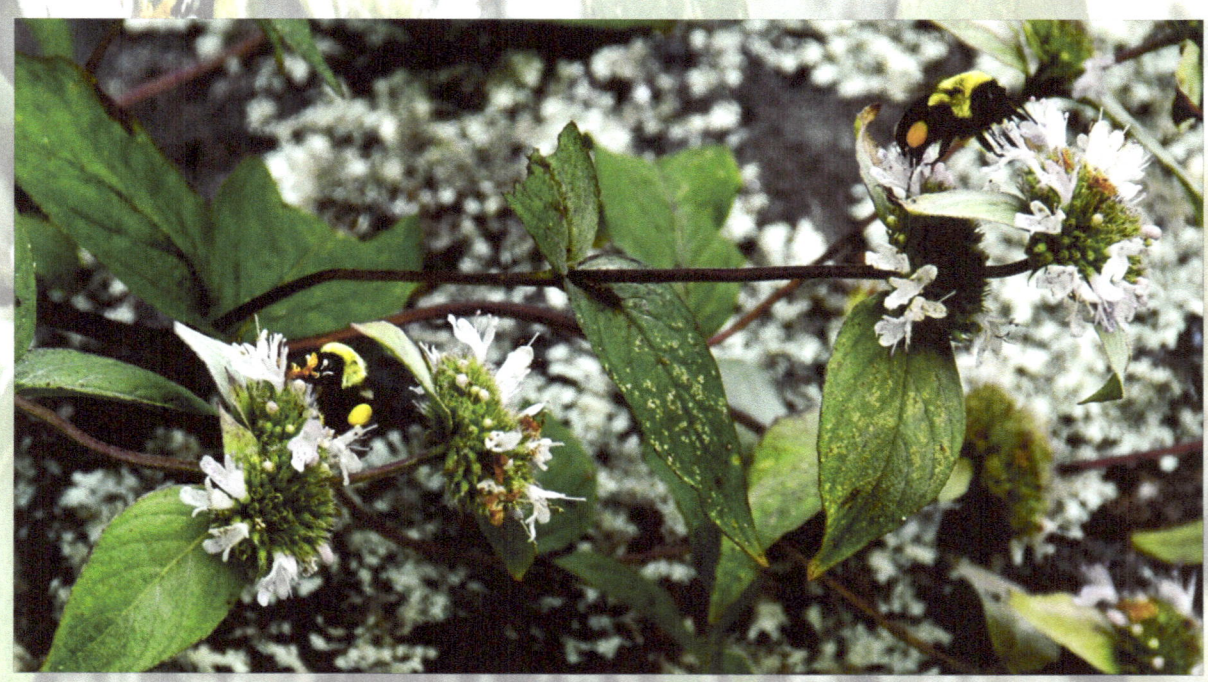

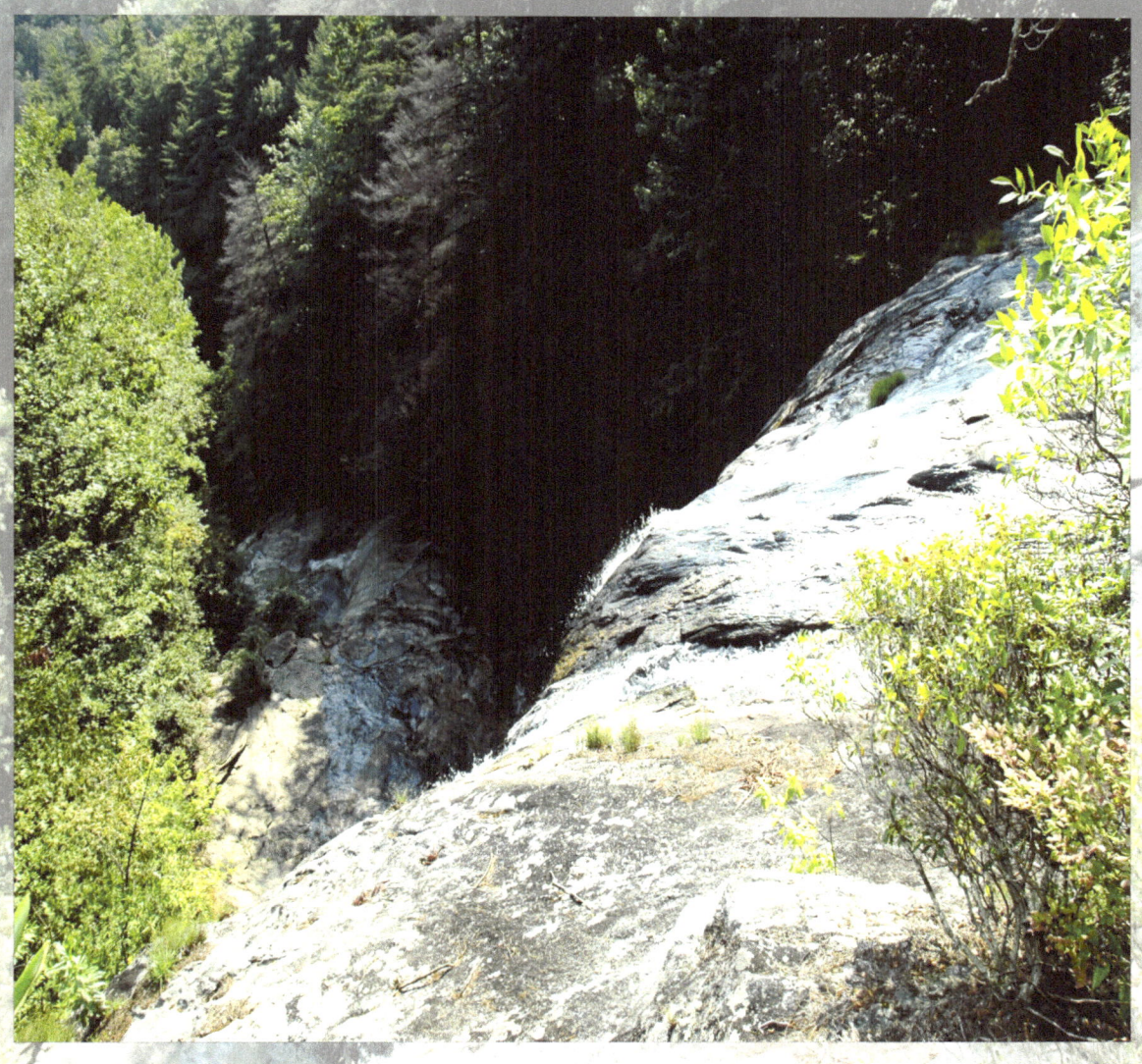

As I near the waterfall, the sounds of the flow, at first
a soft lilt of babble, turns into a deafening roar.
The water spills over the chasm, only to stumble
of the rocks below to commence its voyage to the sea,
creating enchanting music along the way.

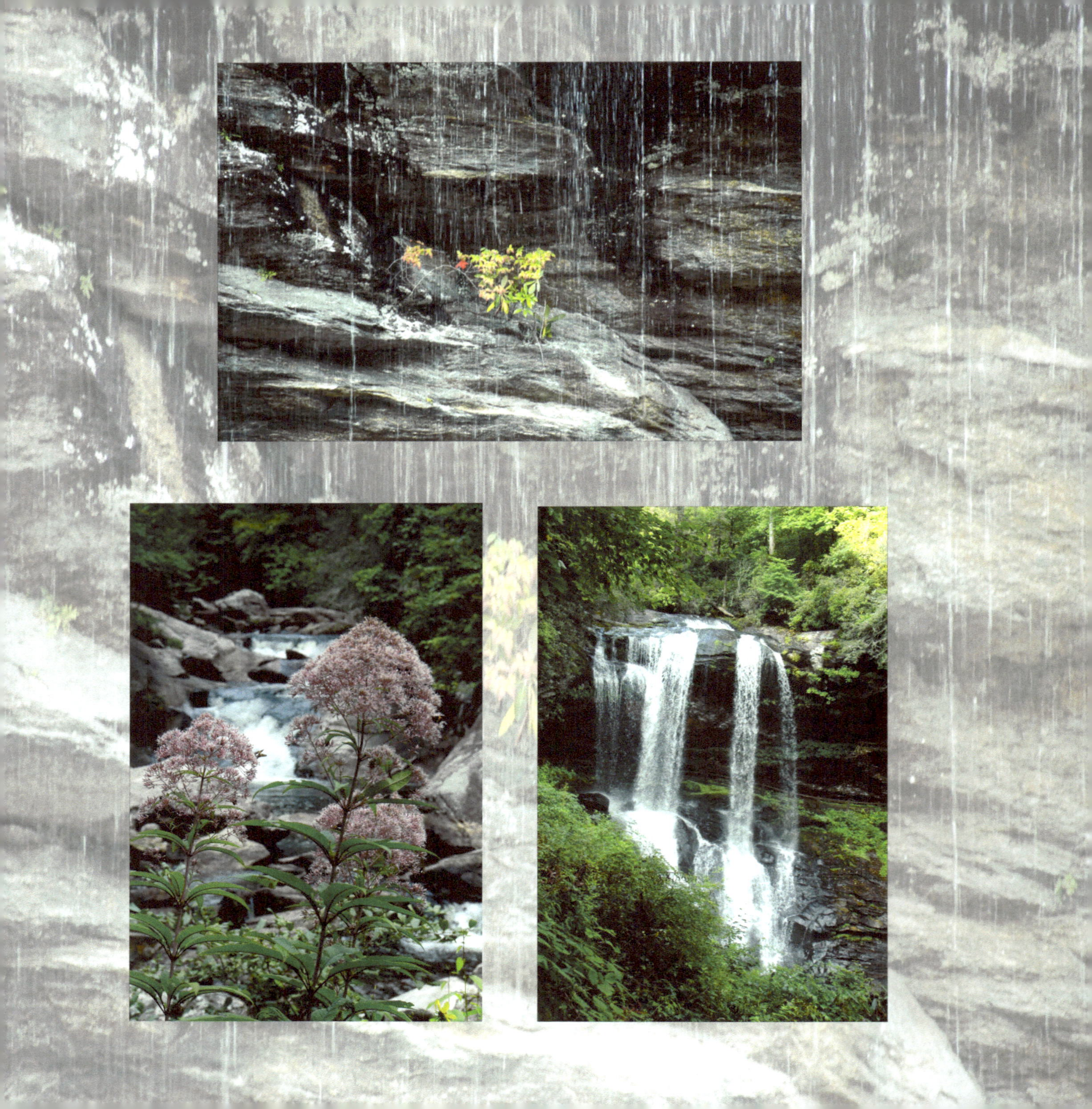

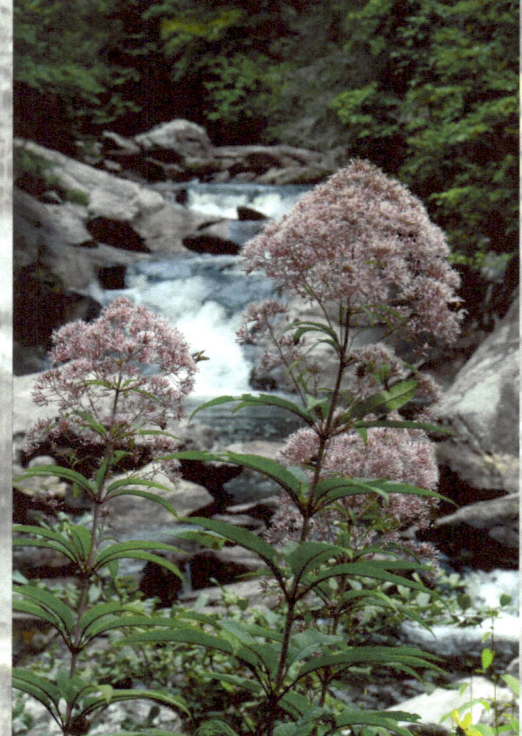
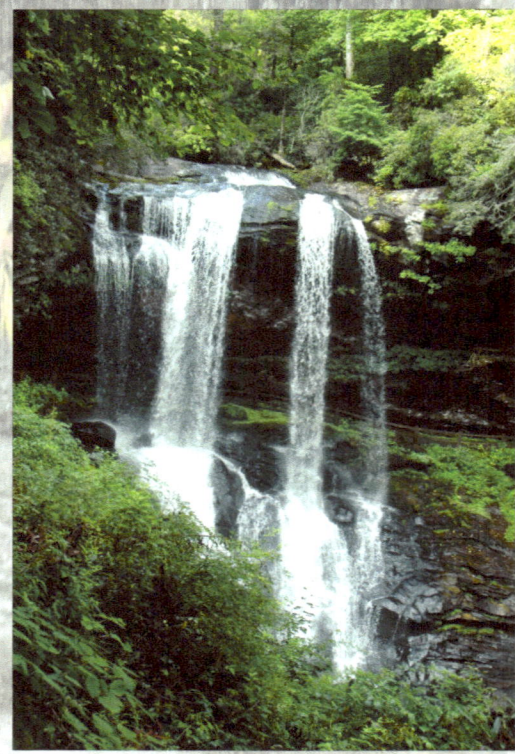

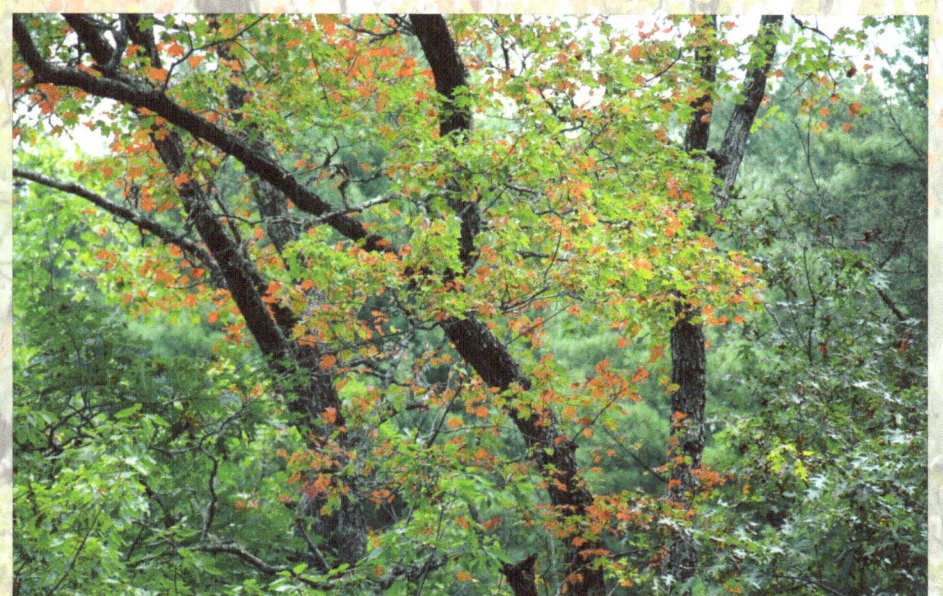

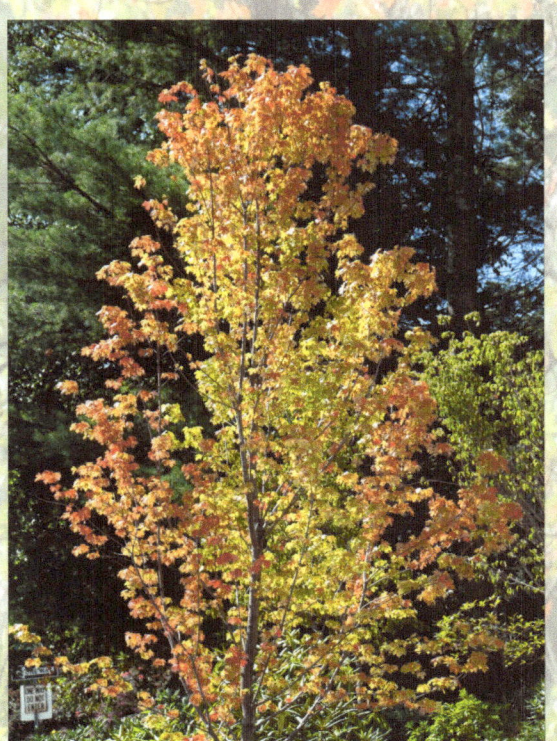

August is still donning its summer coat
but the trees, perched high on the mountain,
know that it will soon be fall.
The leaves are beginning to dress up
for the celebration of life's ever renewing
cycle, one that ends in their demise, but in a
magnificent show of light and color.

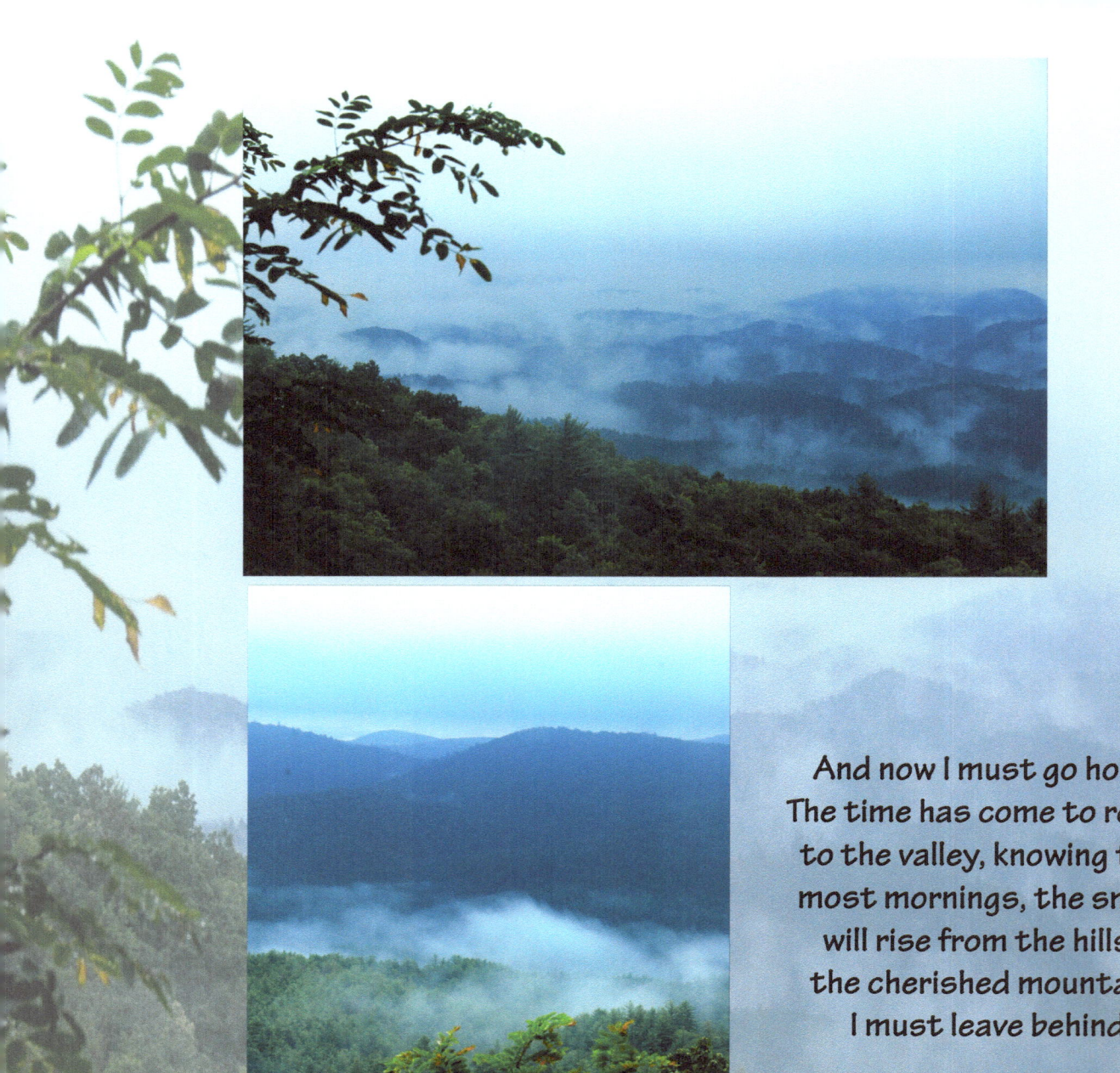

And now I must go home.
The time has come to return
to the valley, knowing that
most mornings, the smoke
will rise from the hills of
the cherished mountains
I must leave behind.

When communing with nature,
remember the most fundamental
laws of the world we live in:

Every living being is worthy of respect and dignity.
Each person deserves equality in social, political and legal realms.
Everyone must be accepted and loved for who they are,
not whom we want them to be, regardless of race, religion,
nationality or social status,
All must be free to seek their personal truth in their own way.
Our goal, as fellow humans, should be peace, liberty, and justice for all,
and a nurturing respect for the natural wonders that surround us,
wherever our footsteps may take us.

When you walk those mountain trails,
remember to only leave your footsteps
and keep the beauty of it all in your soul.